PIANO / VOCAL / CHORDS

EAGLES

hell freezes over

Editor: Tom Roed

ISBN 0-89724-559-8

contents

get over it

Words and Music by
DON HENLEY & GLENN FREY

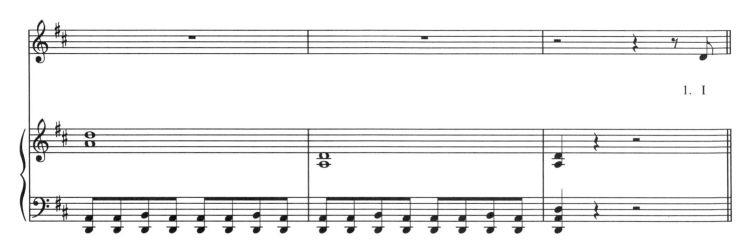

Get Over It - 6 - 1

6

8

Verse 2:
You say you haven't been the same since you had your little crash
But you might feel better if they gave you some cash.
The more I think about it, old Billy was right.
Let's kill all the lawyers, kill 'em tonight.
You don't want to work, you want to live like a king
But the big bad world doesn't owe you a thing.
(To Chorus:)

Chorus 2:
Get over it,
Get over it.
If you don't want to play, then you might as well split.
Get over it, get over it.

Verse 3:
You drag it around like a ball and chain,
You wallow in the guilt, you wallow in the pain.
You wave it like a flag, you wear it like a crown,
Got your mind in the gutter bringin' everybody down.
You bitch about the present, you blame it on the past.
I'd like to find your inner child and kick it's little ass.
(To Chorus:)

Chorus 3:
Get over it.
Get over it.
All this bitchin', and moanin', and pitchin' a fit.
Get over it, get over it.

love will keep us alive

Words and Music by
JIM CAPALDI, PETER VALE
and PAUL CARRACK

Moderately slow ♩ = 88

(with pedal)

Verses 1 - 3:

1.4. I was

stand - ing,___	all a - lone___ a - gainst the world out - side.___
wor - ry,___	some - times you've just___ got to let it ride.___
found___ you,___	there's no more___ emp - ti - ness in - side.___

Love Will Keep Us Alive - 5 - 1

the girl from yesterday

Words and Music by
GLENN FREY and JACK TEMPCHIN

He packed his things,_ walked out the door_ and drove a - way._
how some - one who_ had been so close_ could be so far_ a - way._

And she be - came_ the girl from yes - ter - day.___

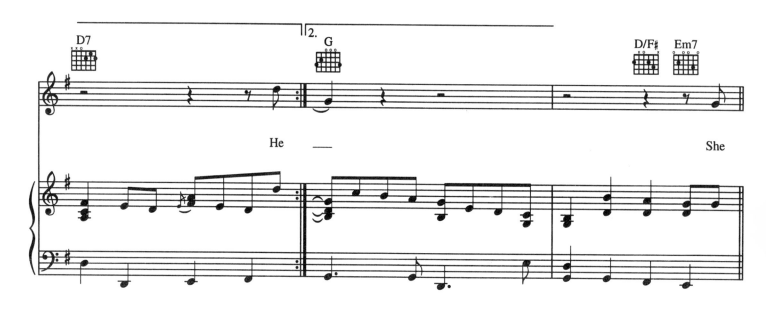

He ___ She

18

learn to be still

Words and Music by
DON HENLEY and
STAN LYNCH

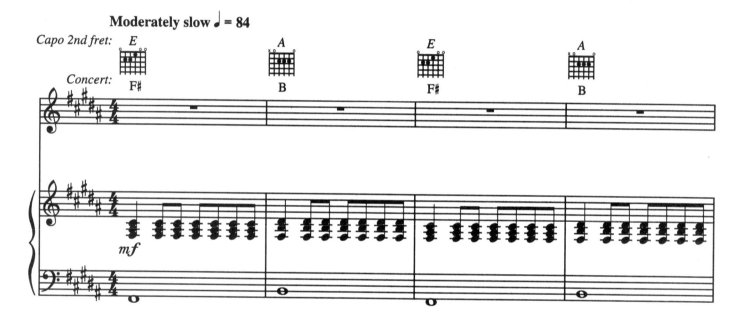

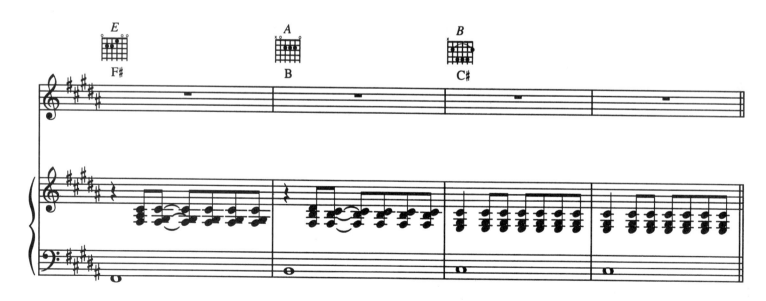

May-be you've_ for - got-ten the heav-en ly - ing at__ your_

__ feet. Yeah,_ yeah, yeah._

tequila sunrise

Words and Music by
DON HENLEY & GLENN FREY

Tequila Sunrise - 5 - 1

hotel california

Words and Music by
DON HENLEY, GLENN FREY
and DON FELDER

Hotel California - 7 - 1

wasted time

Words and Music by
DON HENLEY and GLENN FREY

Wasted Time - 6 - 1

42

time. Ooh, _____ an-oth-er love___ has come and gone.___

Ooh, _____ and the years___ keep rush-ing on. _____ I re-

mem-ber what you told__ me be-fore you went out on__ your own:__ "Some-times to

keep it __ to-geth-er, we got to leave it a-lone." ___ So

Wasted Time - 6 - 5

pretty maids all in a row

Words and Music by
JOE WALSH and JOE VITALE

Pretty Maids All in a Row - 4 - 4

i can't tell you why

Words and Music by
DON HENLEY, GLENN FREY & TIMOTHY B. SCHMIT

Moderately slow

Look at us, ba - by, up all night _ tear - in' our love _ a - part. _

Instrumental

Aren't we the same _ two peo - ple who lived _ through years _

in the dark? Oh. _

Ev -'ry time I try to

I Can't Tell You Why - 4 - 2

I Can't Tell You Why - 4 - 4

new york minute

Words and Music by
DON HENLEY, DANNY KORTCHMAR
and JAI WINDING

Slowly, with a heavy beat

1. Har - ry got__ up dressed all in black,
4. I pulled my coat a - round my shoul - ders__ and took a walk down through the park.

New York Minute - 7 - 1

2. He had a home ___ the love of a girl ___
3. Ly - ing here in the dark - ness I hear the si - rens wail.
5. What the head makes cloud - y the heart makes ver - y clear.

but men get ___ lost some - times ___ as years un - furl. ___
Some - bod - y go - in' to e - mer - gen - cy, ___ some - bod - y go - in' to jail. ___ If you
The days were so much bright - er ___ In the time when she was here. ___ But I ___

One day he crossed some line ___ and he was too much ___ in this world. ___ But I
find some - bod - y to love in this world you bet - ter hang on ___ tooth and nail. ___ The wolf is
___ know there's some - bod - y some - where make these dark clouds dis - ap - pear. Un - til that

New York min-ute.

And in these days

when dark-ness falls_ ear-ly, and peo-ple rush home

to the ones they love_ you bet-ter take a fools_ ad-vice

and take care of your own.   'Cause one day they're here, __ next day they're

gone.   *(Muted trumpet solo - ad lib.)*

D.S. %al Coda

the last resort

Words and Music by
DON HENLEY and GLENN FREY

The Last Resort - 6 - 1

The Last Resort - 6 - 2

The Last Resort - 6 - 6

take it easy

Words and Music by
JACKSON BROWNE & GLENN FREY

Take It Easy - 6 - 1

Take It Easy - 6 - 3

Take It Easy - 6 - 5

in the city

Words and Music by
JOE WALSH and BARRY DE VORZON

In the City - 4 - 1

life in the fast lane

Words and Music by
DON HENLEY, GLENN FREY
and JOE WALSH

Moderate rock ♩ = 110

He was a

Life in the Fast Lane - 8 - 1

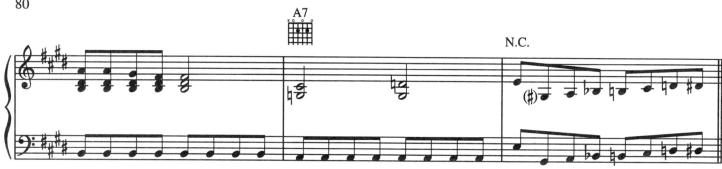

Blow-in' and burn - in',   blind-ed by thirst,_   they__ did-n't see the   stop_ sign; took a turn_

desperado

Words and Music by
DON HENLEY and GLENN FREY

Desperado, why don't you come to your senses? You been out ridin' fences for

Desperado - 6 - 1

84

Desperado - 6 - 2